Contents

Introduction

Welcome to *Music Theory in Practice Model Answers*, Grade 4. These answers are a useful resource to help you prepare for ABRSM Theory of Music exams. This book is designed to be used alongside the revised *Music Theory in Practice* workbook (published 2008).

All the answers in this book would receive full marks in an exam. Accepted options are included for cases where an answer may be expressed in more than one way. For composition-style questions, a model answer is provided as an example of good practice.

Using these answers

- Answers are given in the same order and, where possible, in the same layout as in the corresponding *Music Theory in Practice* workbook. This makes it easy to match the answers to the questions.
- Where it is necessary to show the answer on a stave, the original stave is printed in grey with the answer shown in black, for example:

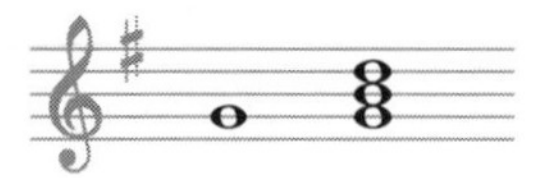

- Alternative answers are separated by an oblique stroke (/) or by *or*, for example:

B / B♮ / B natural

- Answers that require the candidate to write out a scale or chord have been shown at one octave only. Reasonable alternatives at different octaves can also receive full marks.

First published in 2009 by ABRSM (Publishing) Ltd, a wholly owned subsidiary of ABRSM

Typeset by Barnes Music Engraving Ltd
Cover by Økvik Design
Inside design by Vermillion
Printed in England by Caligraving Ltd, Thetford, Norfolk

Time signatures

Exercise 4
(a)
Adagio molto
Beethoven
p
(b)
(Maestoso)
Brahms
p
(c)
Handel
(d)
Andante tranquillo
Warlock
mp
(e)
(Allegro)
Brahms
p
Exercise 5
(a)
(b)
(c)
(d)
(e)
Exercise 6
(a)
Andante
Wagner
p
or
(b)
(Andante)
Handel
(c)
(Allegro)
Hindemith
or
p
(d)
Allegro molto moderato
Sibelius
mp cresc.
f
or
(e)
Allegro
J. S. Bach

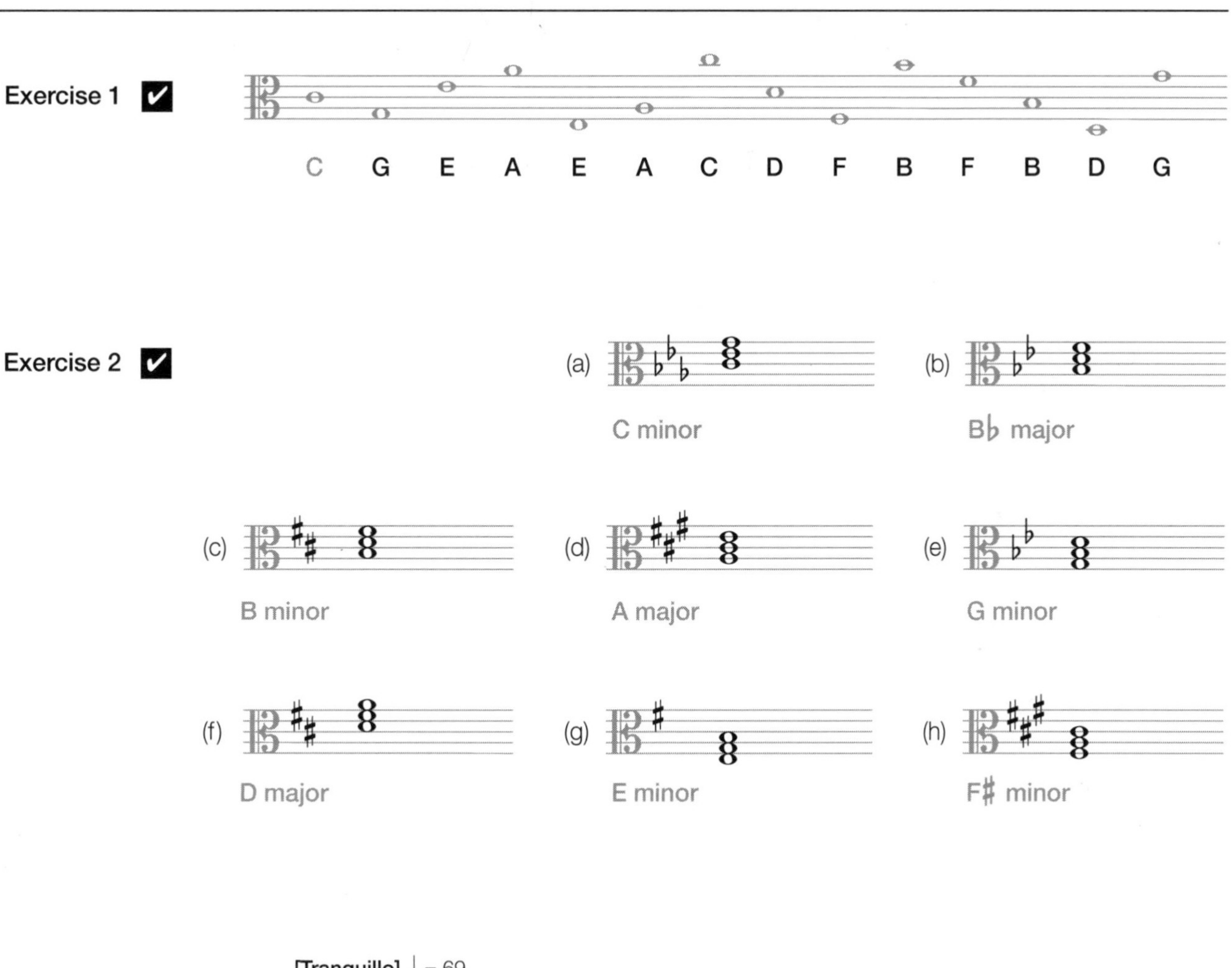
Exercise 1
C G E A E A C D F B F B D G
Exercise 2
(a)
C minor
(b)
B♭ major
(c)
B minor
(d)
A major
(e)
G minor
(f)
D major
(g)
E minor
(h)
F♯ minor

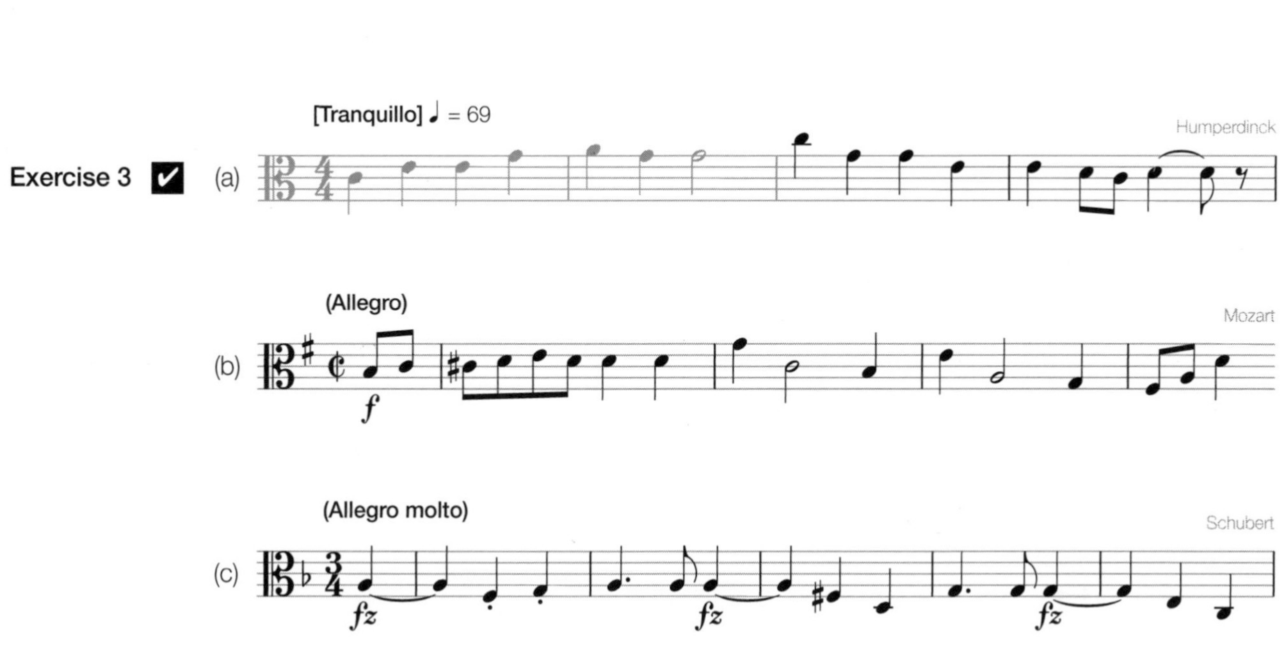
Exercise 3
(a)
[Tranquillo] ♩ = 69
Humperdinck
(b)
(Allegro)
Mozart
f
(c)
(Allegro molto)
Schubert
fz
fz
fz

Exercise 4

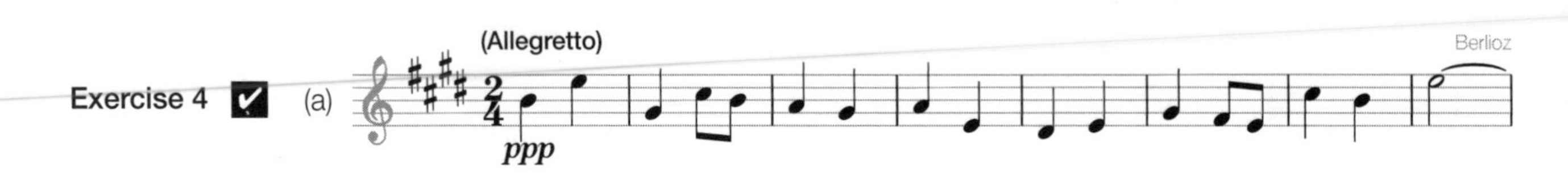

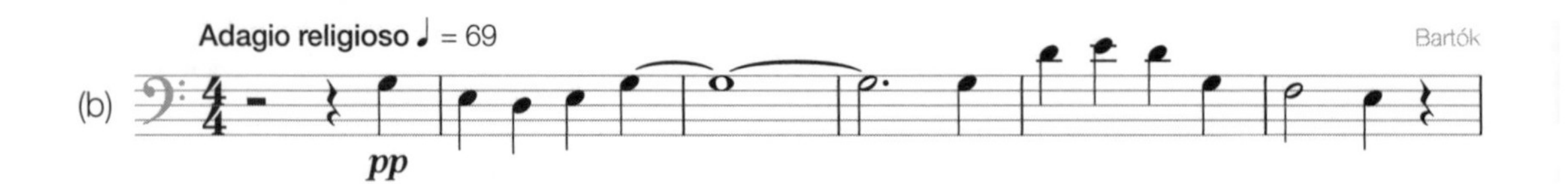

Double sharps and double flats

Exercise 1

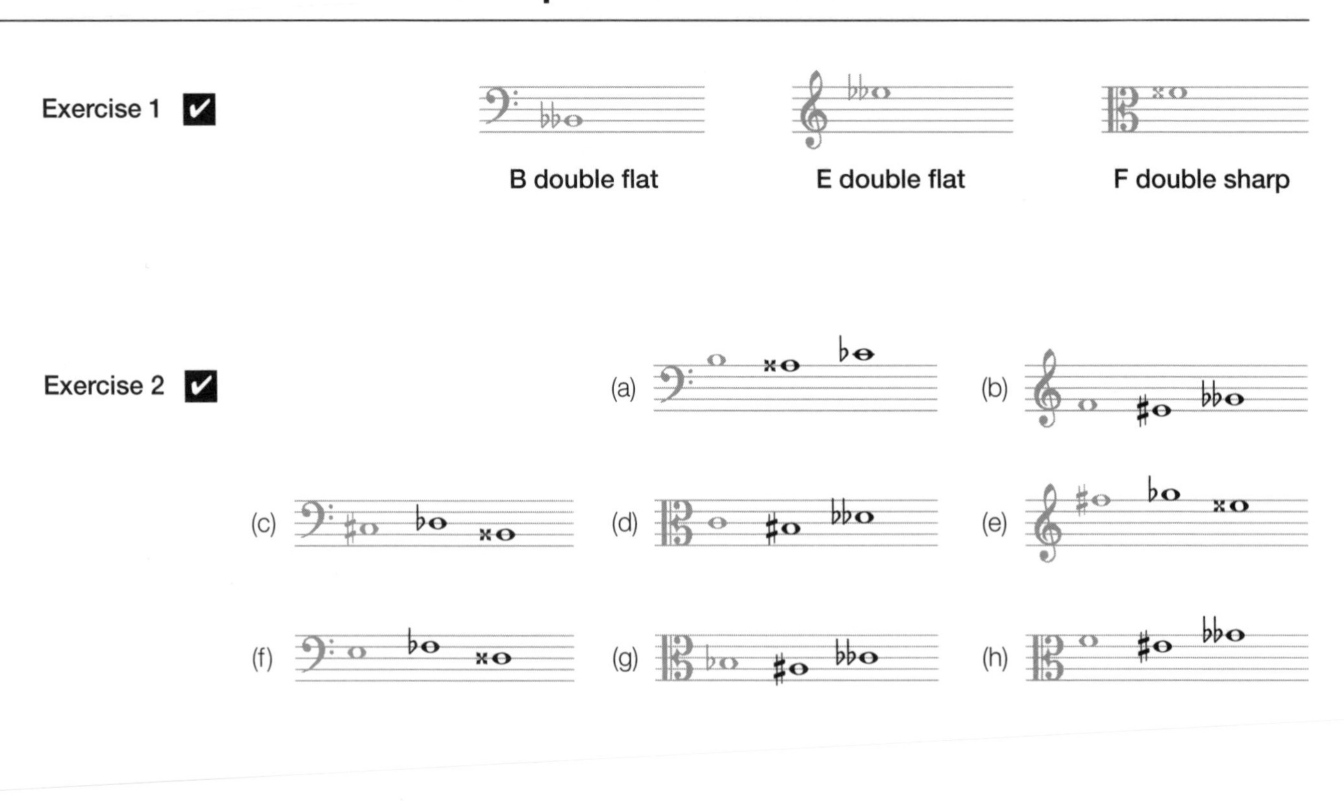

Exercise 2

Exercise 3

Breves (double whole notes), double dots, duplets

Keys with five sharps or flats
Technical names of notes in diatonic scales

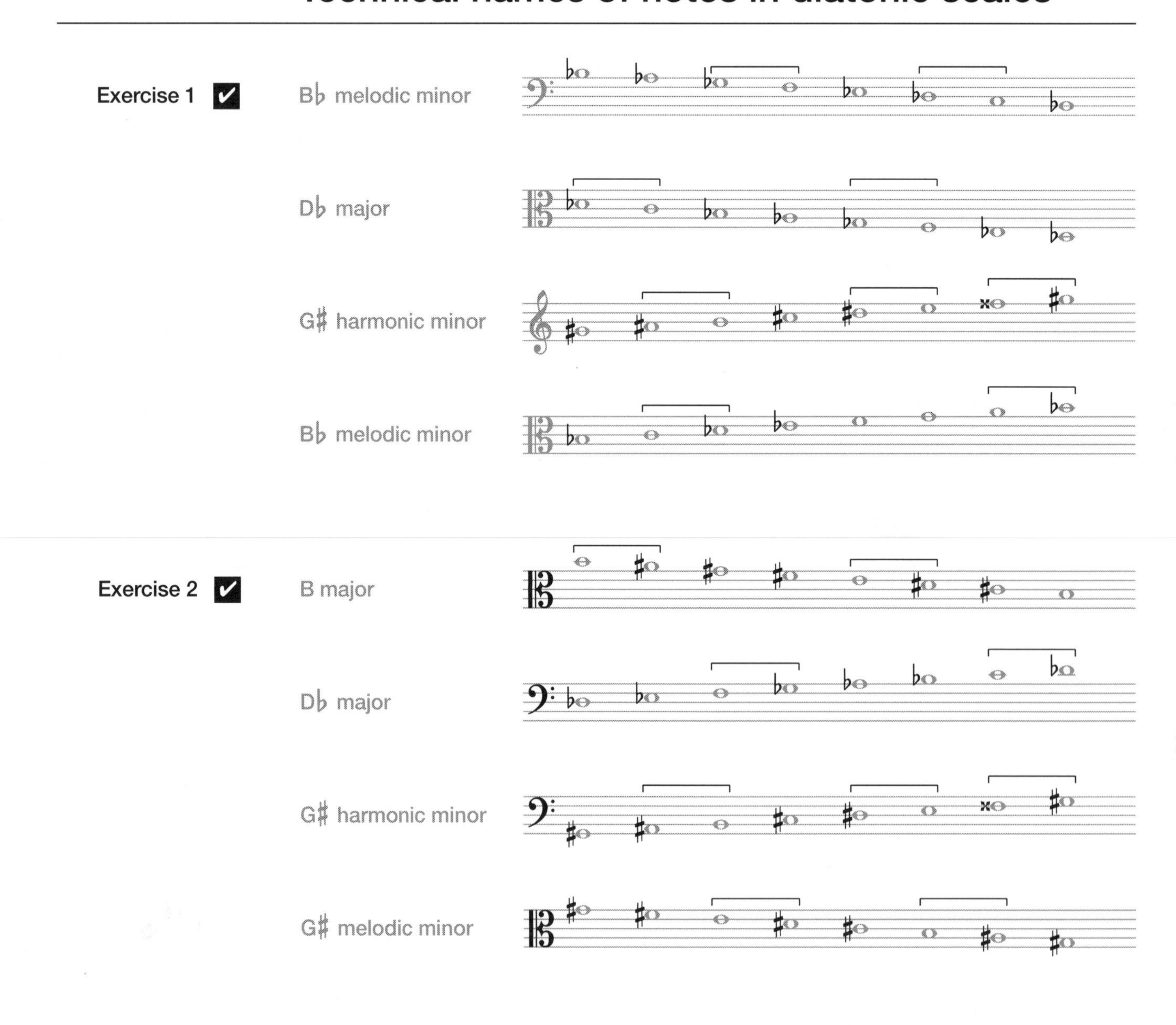

Exercise 3
B♭ minor
G♯ minor
D♭ major
D♭ major
B major
B major
G♯ minor
G♯ minor
B♭ minor
D♭ major
B♭ minor
Exercise 4
Key B♭ minor
Andantino
Tchaikovsky
(a)
p
Key G♯ minor
J. S. Bach
(b)
Key F minor
Allegretto
Beethoven
(c)
p
Key B major
♩ = 72
Stravinsky
(d)
mf

Key E major
Andante sostenuto ♩ = 52
Berlioz
(e)
mf

Exercise 5 ✔

(a) Key **A major**
1 **mediant** 3 **supertonic**
2 **leading note** 4 **subdominant**

(b) Key **D♭ major**
1 **mediant** 3 **subdominant**
2 **leading note** 4 **dominant**

(c) Key **E♭ major**
1 **dominant** 3 **subdominant**
2 **supertonic** 4 **tonic**

(d) Key **B major**
1 **supertonic** 3 **submediant**
2 **dominant** 4 **mediant**

(e) Key **F minor**
1 **leading note** 3 **submediant**
2 **subdominant** 4 **mediant**

(f) Key **B♭ minor**
1 **supertonic** 3 **subdominant**
2 **submediant** 4 **leading note**

Four-bar rhythms

Exercise 1 ✔

There are many ways of completing this exercise. The specimen answers that follow provide examples of good practice.

(a)

(b)

(c)

(d)

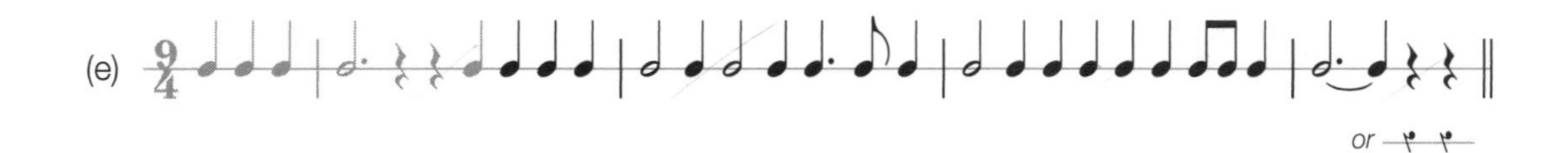

(f)

(g)

(h)

Exercise 2 ✓

There are many ways of completing this exercise. The specimen answers that follow provide examples of good practice.

(b) 3

(c) 2

(d) or or

(e)

(f)

Triads and chords on I, IV and V

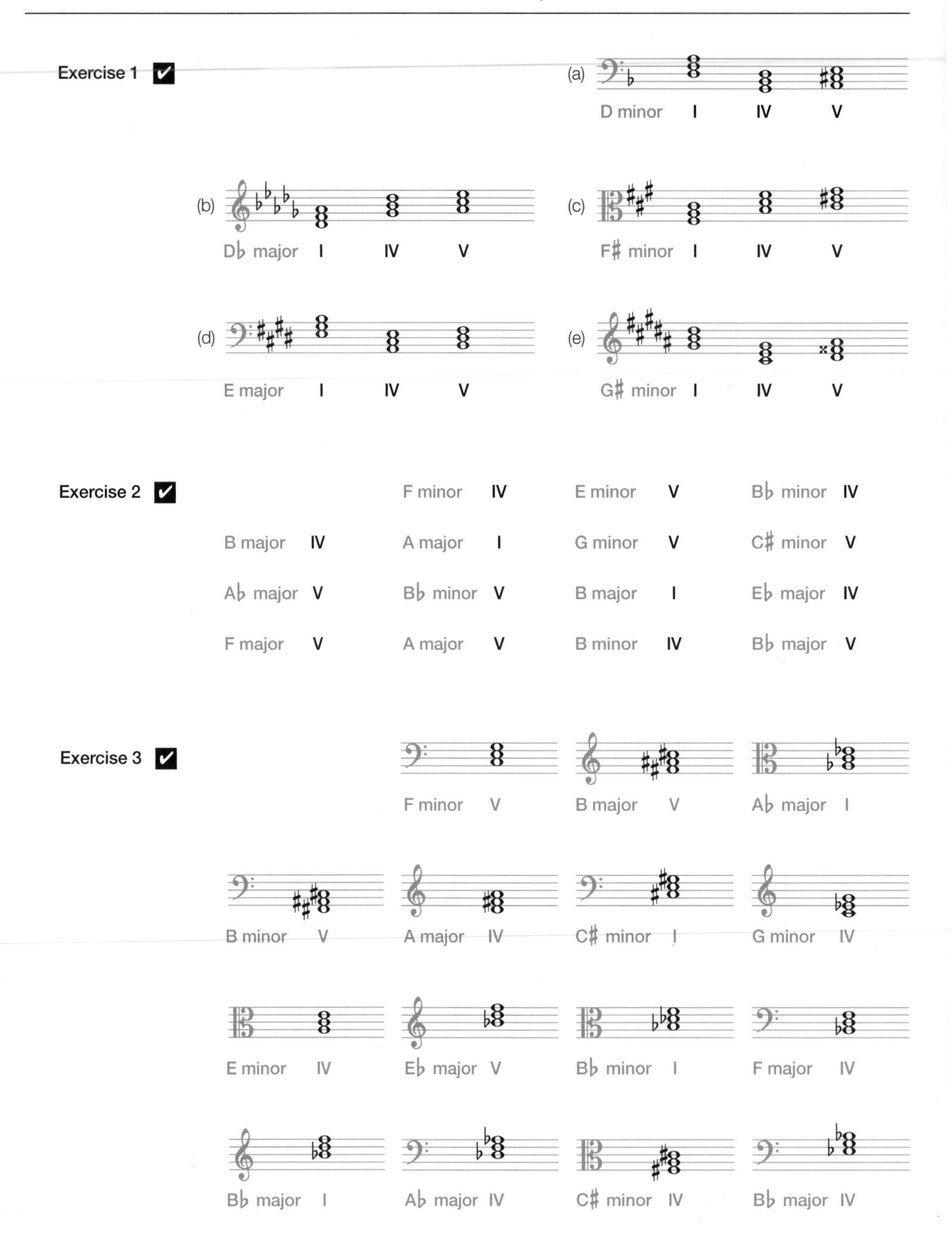

Exercise 4 ✔

	Key			
* (a)	Key	G major	I	IV	V
(b)	Key	E major	IV	V	I
(c)	Key	A major	V	IV	I
(d)	Key	C minor	IV	I	V
(e)	Key	E major	IV	V	I
* (f)	Key	D♭ major	IV	I	V
(g)	Key	B minor	IV	I	V
(h)	Key	E minor	IV	V	I

Intervals

Exercise 1 ✔

	perfect 5th	minor 6th	diminished 5th
minor 3rd	major 6th	minor 7th	augmented 4th
minor 3rd	diminished 7th	major 7th	minor 2nd
minor 3rd	diminished 4th	major 7th	augmented 5th
diminished 5th	perfect 4th	major 6th	diminished 7th
augmented 4th	major 2nd	diminished 4th	minor 7th

Exercise 2 ✔

(a)	1 minor 3rd	2 major 3rd	3 major 6th	4 perfect 4th
(b)	1 perfect 4th	2 minor 3rd	3 minor 7th	4 major 3rd
(c)	1 major 6th	2 perfect 5th	3 minor 3rd	4 major 6th
(d)	1 major 3rd	2 perfect 4th	3 diminished 7th	4 minor 2nd

* For editions printed in 2008, the answers relate to the following chords in the music:
Ex. 4 (a): bar 1, beat 1; bar 2, beat 3; bar 4, beat 1.
Ex. 4 (f): bar 1, beat 2; bar 2, beat 1; bar 3, beat 2.

Writing a rhythm to words

Exercise 1 ✔ There are many ways of completing this exercise. The specimen answers that follow provide examples of good practice.

(a) **Either:** Words by John Masefield

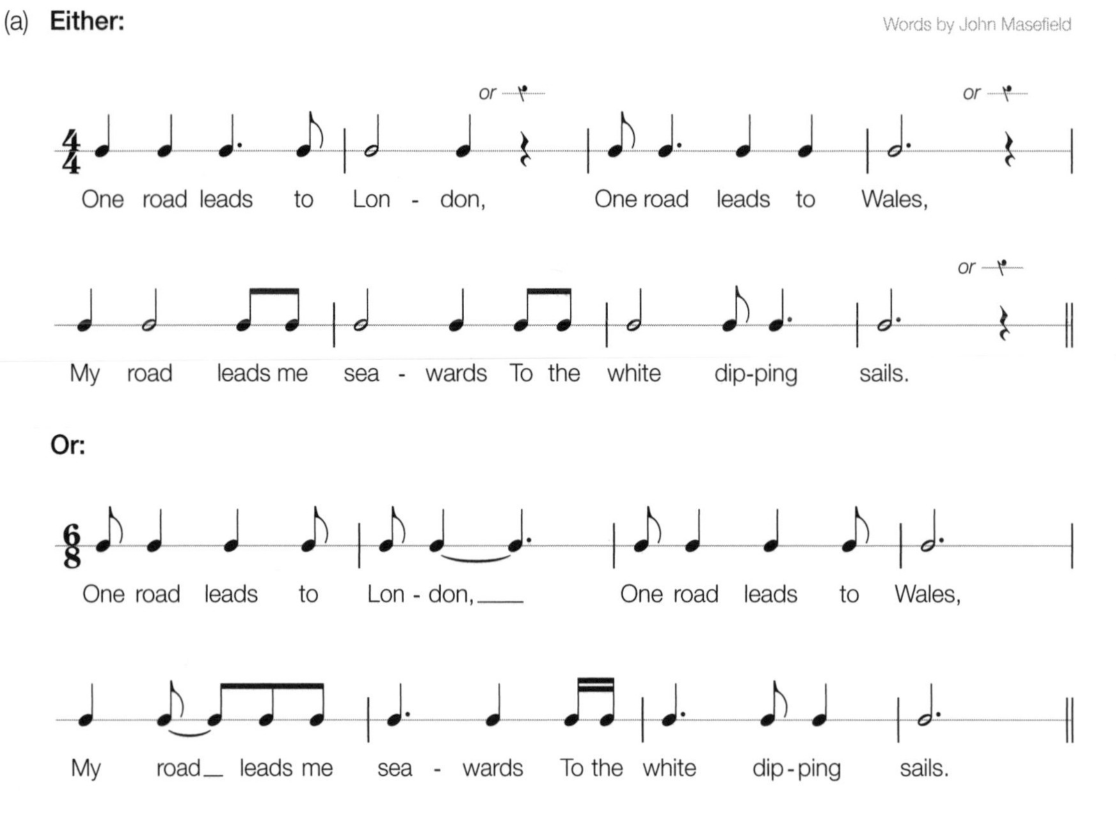

(b) **Either:** Words by William Jay Smith

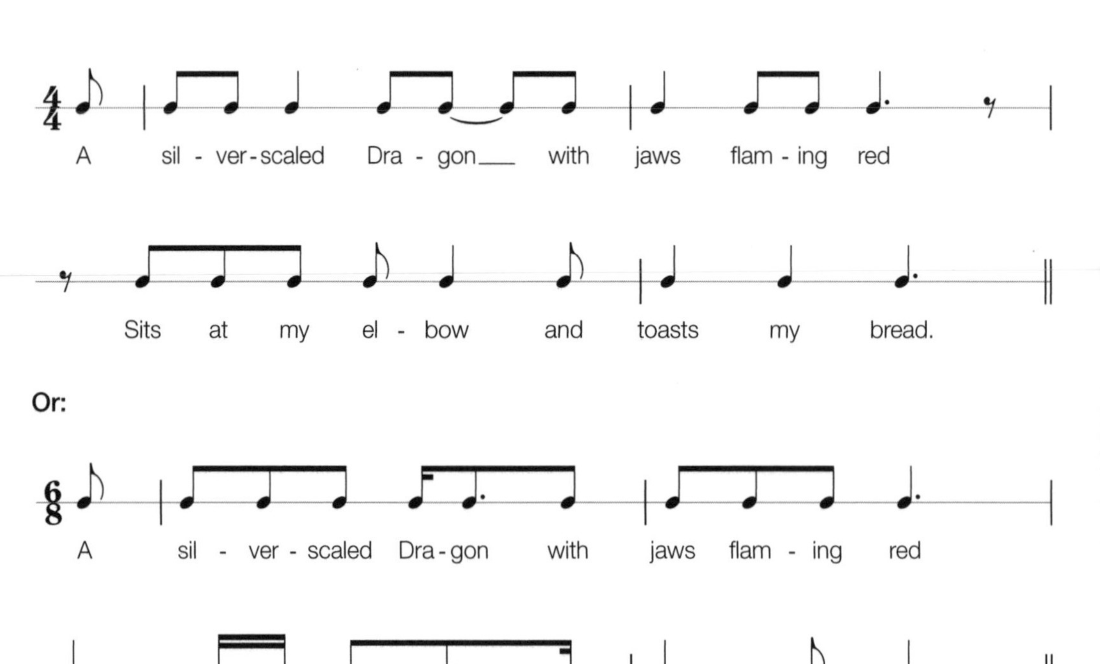

(c) **Either:**

Words by Thomas Hood

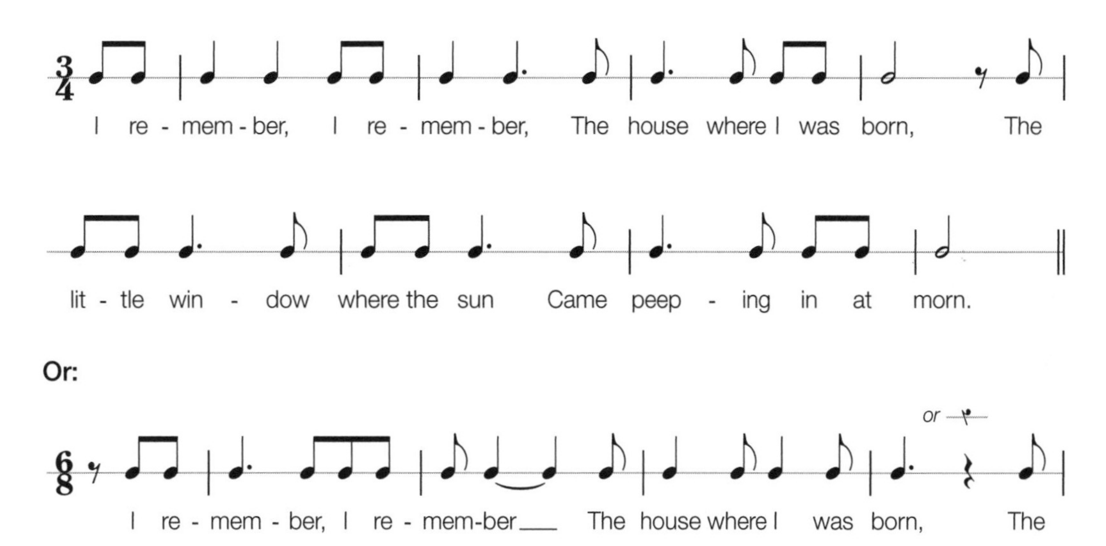

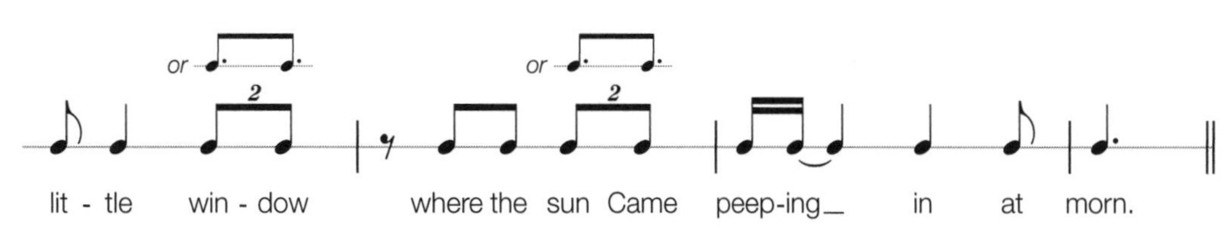

(d) **Either:**

Traditional

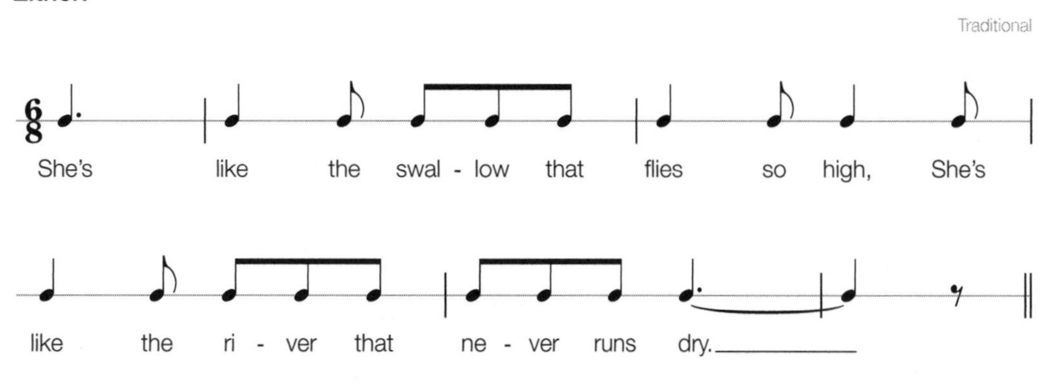

Or:

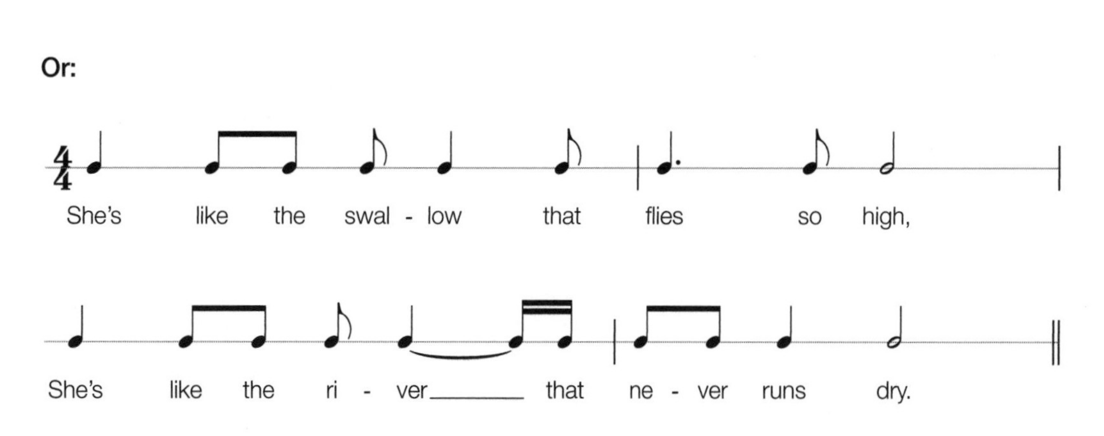

(e) **Either:**

Words by Robert Louis Stevenson

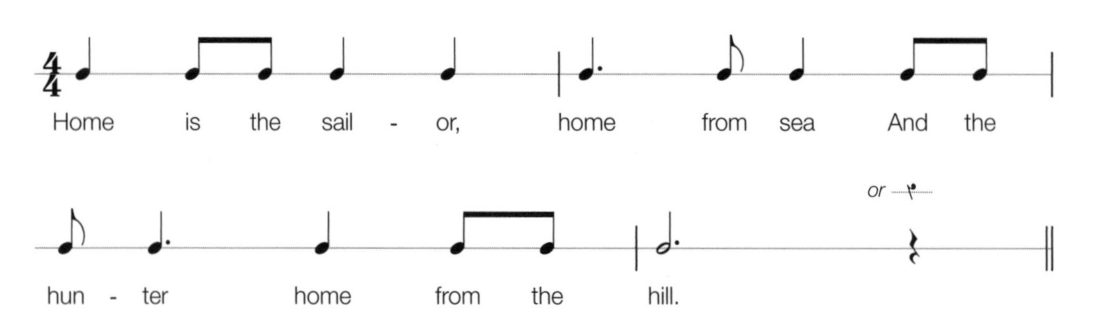

Or:

Home is the sail - or, home from sea And the

hun - ter home from the hill.

(f) **Either:**

Words by Christina Rossetti

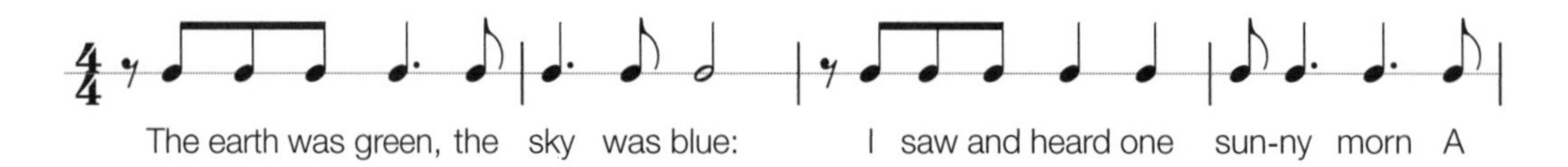

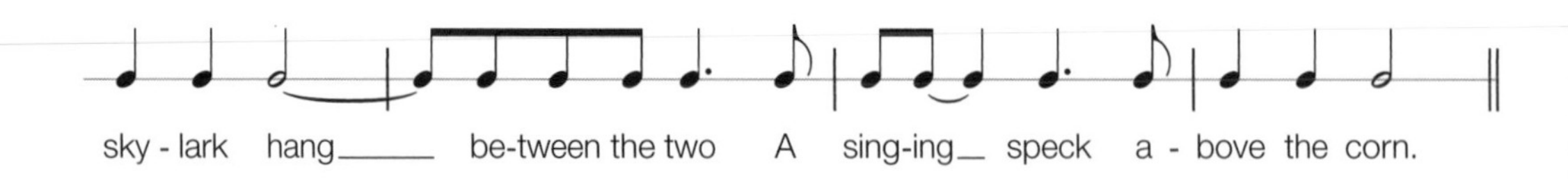

Or:

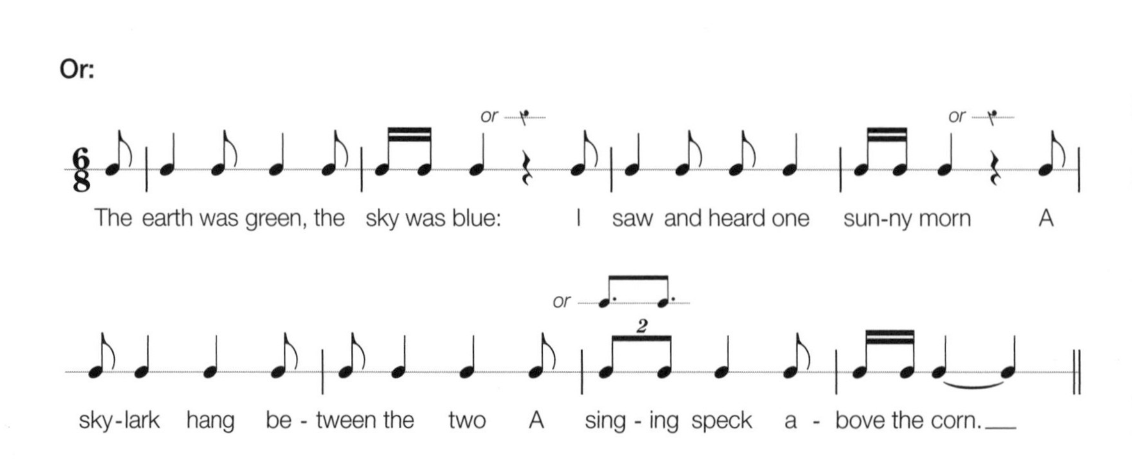

The chromatic scale

Exercise 3 ✔

Ornaments

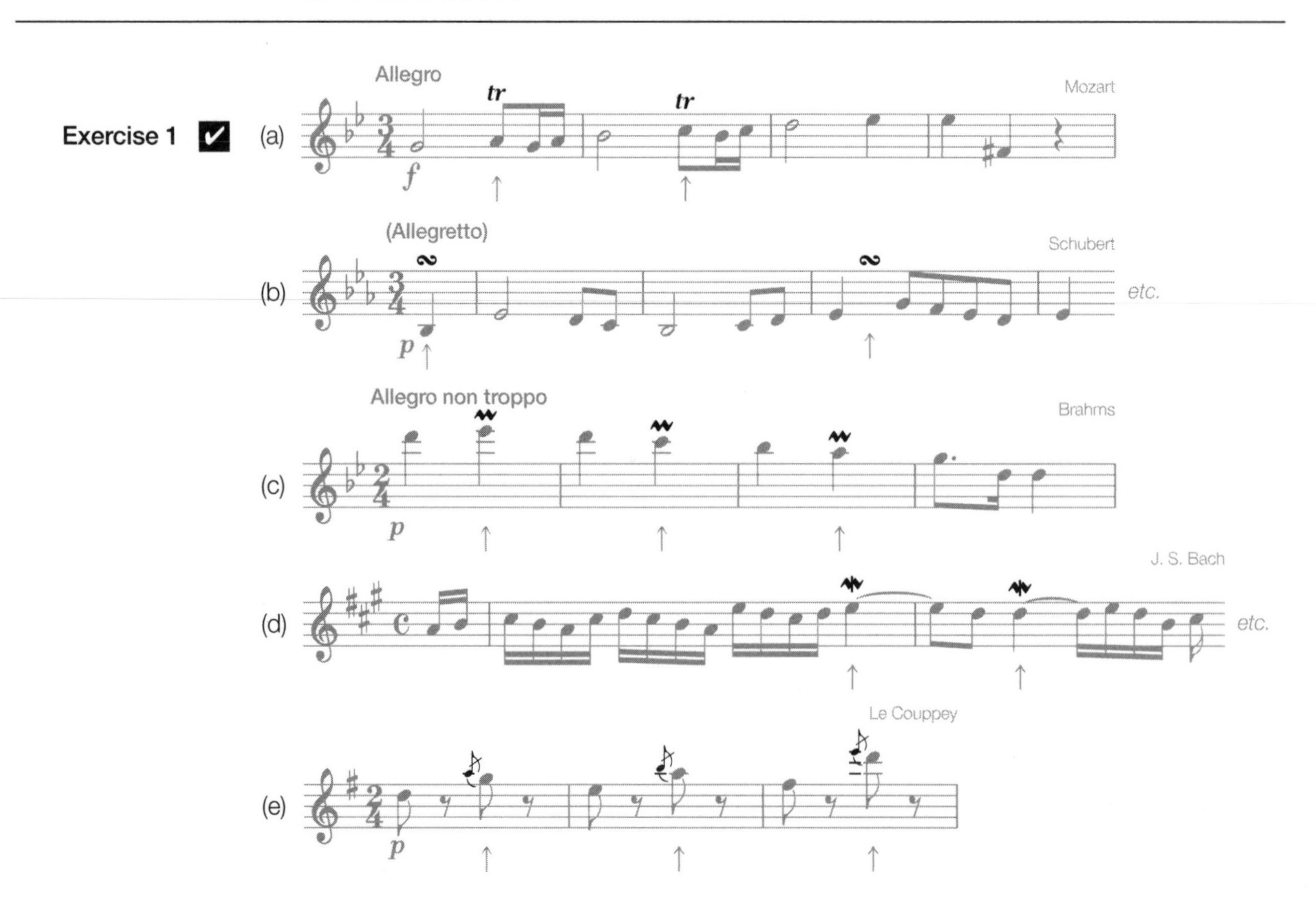

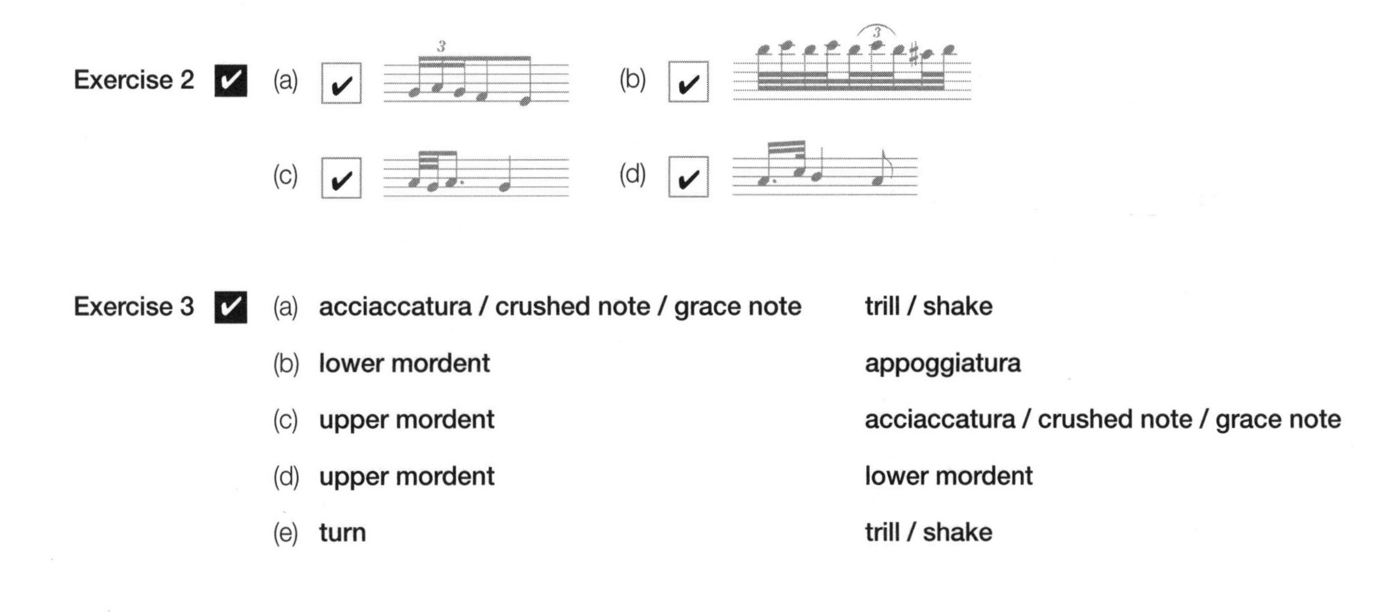

Exercise 2 (a) ✔ (b) ✔ (c) ✔ (d) ✔

Exercise 3 (a) **acciaccatura / crushed note / grace note** **trill / shake**

(b) **lower mordent** **appoggiatura**

(c) **upper mordent** **acciaccatura / crushed note / grace note**

(d) **upper mordent** **lower mordent**

(e) **turn** **trill / shake**

General exercises

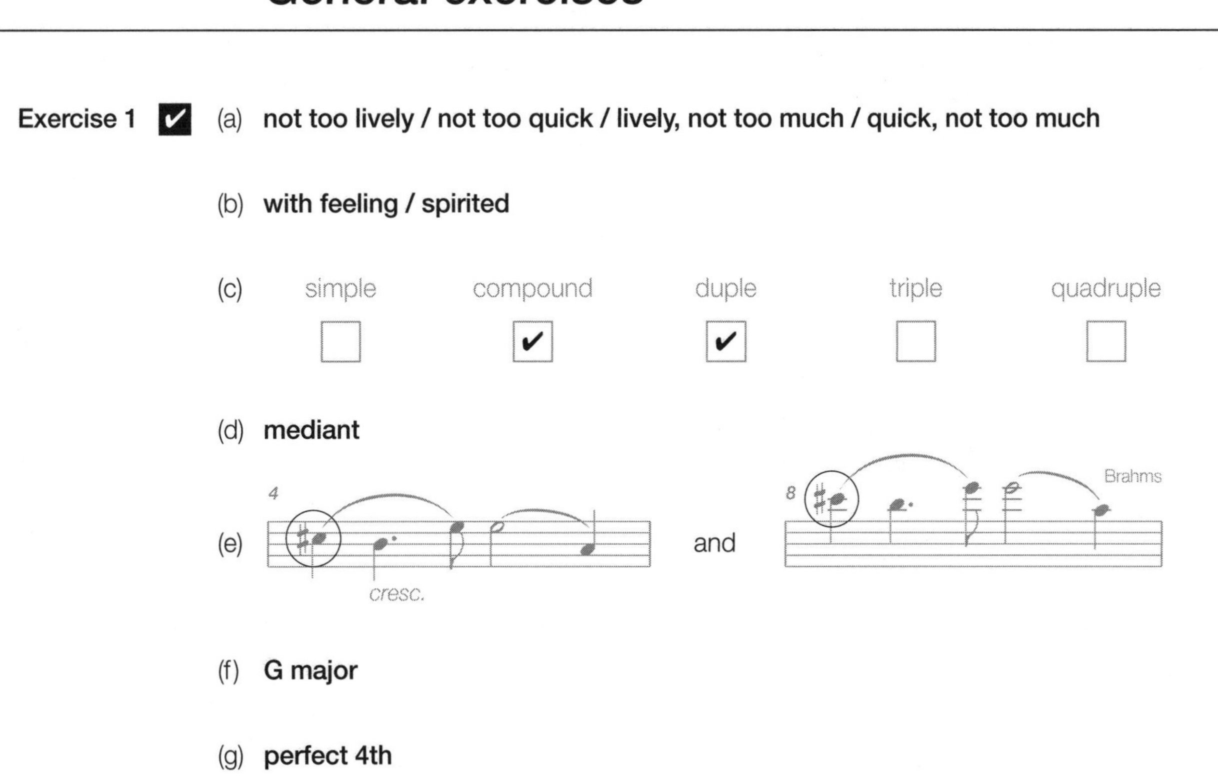

Exercise 1 (a) **not too lively / not too quick / lively, not too much / quick, not too much**

(b) **with feeling / spirited**

(c) simple ☐ compound ✔ duple ✔ triple ☐ quadruple ☐

(d) **mediant**

(e) [music] and [music]

(f) **G major**

(g) **perfect 4th**

(h) getting softer ☐ getting louder ✔ staying the same ☐

(i) **same rhythm / same melodic shape / bars 5–8 are an octave higher**

(j) **viola / cello / double bass**

(k)

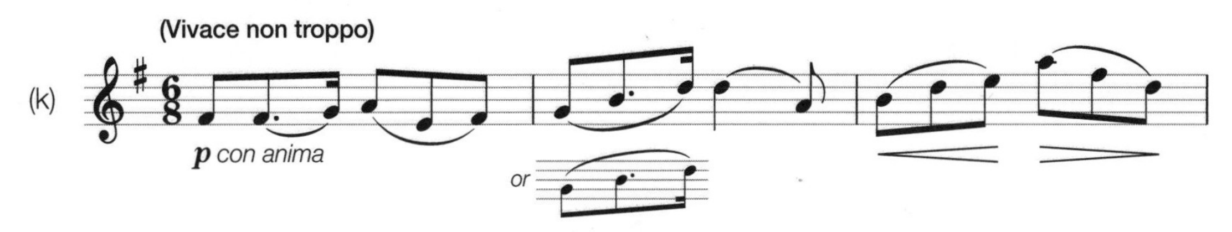

Exercise 2 ☑ (a) **slower**

più means 'more' which suggests a comparison of speed

(b)

(c) **D♭ major**

(d) **B double flat**

(e) **F sharp / E double sharp**

(f) **minor 2nd**

(g) **descending notes in stepwise movement / the notes go down in steps**

(h) **upper mordent**

(i)

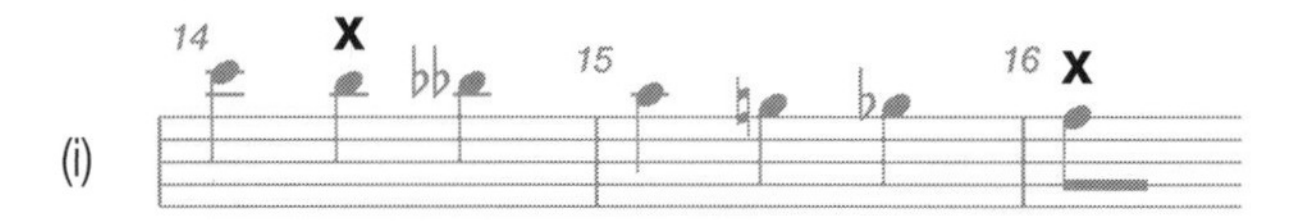

(j) **flute / oboe / clarinet**

(k)

Exercise 3 ✔ (a) simple ☑ compound ☐ duple ☑ triple ☐ quadruple ☐

(b) **espressivo** **expressive / expressively**

(c) **perfect 4th**

(d) **viola** **violas use the alto clef**

(e) **articulation / slurring; dynamics / decrescendo; rhythm / crotchets only**

(f) **slight pressure / emphasis / slight separation**

(g) **9** **D♮ / D natural**

(h)

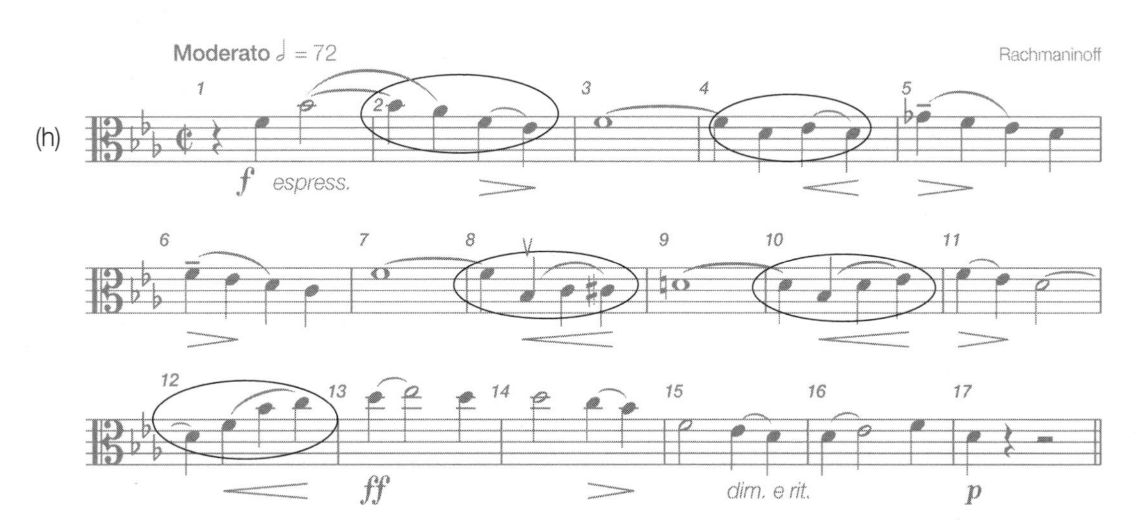

(i) **highest and loudest notes**

(j)

Exercise 4 ✔

(a) **fast walking pace / slow walking pace**
singing
very broadly

(b) **acciaccatura / crushed note / grace note**

(c) ✔ 

(d) Bar 16 **minor 6th** Bar 17 **perfect 4th** Bar 18 **major 3rd**
Bar 19 **diminished 4th** Bar 20 **minor 2nd**

(e) G (bar 12) **subdominant**
C♯ (bar 12) **leading note** E (bar 13) **supertonic** B♭ (bar 13) **submediant**
F (bar 14) **mediant** D (bar 15) **tonic** A (bar 16) **dominant**

(f) **the performance marks are for violin: bowing directions (V and ⊓) and the instruction to play on the G string ('sul G')**

(g) 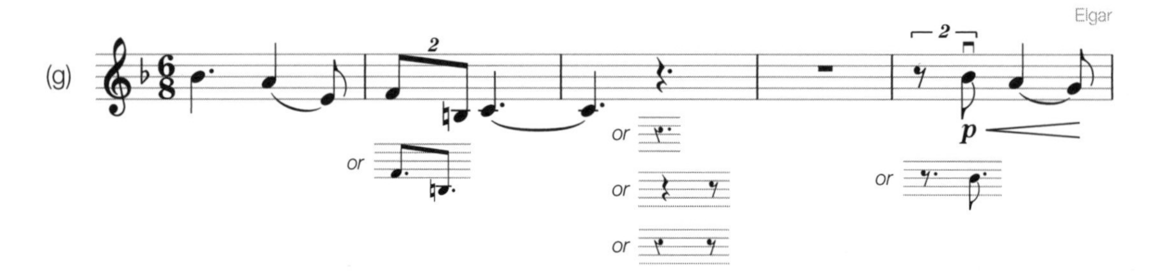

Acknowledgements

Page 3: Howells, *Psalm Preludes for organ*, Op. 32 No. 1
© Novello & Co. Ltd

Page 4: Hindemith, *Ludus Tonalis* ('Interludium')
© 1943 Schott & Co. Ltd, Mainz, Germany
Reproduced by permission. All rights reserved.

Page 4: Sibelius, Symphony No. 7
© Edition Wilhelm Hansen AS

Page 6: Bartók, Piano Concerto No. 3 (2nd mvt)
© Copyright 1947 Hawkes & Son (London) Ltd
Reproduced by permission of Boosey & Hawkes Music Publishers Ltd.

Page 7: Ravel, Sonatine (1st mvt)
Reproduced for sale in France, Belgium, Spain & Italy by permission of Editions Durand S.A. / Universal Music Publishing MGB Ltd.

Page 8: Delius, *Walk to the Paradise Garden*
Reproduced for sale in France, Spain & Mexico by permission of Boosey & Hawkes Music Publishers Ltd.

Page 8: Ravel, String Quartet (2nd mvt)
Reproduced for sale in France, Belgium, Spain & Italy by permission of Editions Durand S.A. / Universal Music Publishing MGB Ltd.

Page 9: Stravinsky, *Firebird* ('Ronde des Princesses')
© 1910 P. Jurgenson, Moscow. © 1933 assigned to B. Schott's Söhne
Reproduced by permission.

Page 14: John Masefield, *Roadways*
Reproduced by permission of The Society of Authors as the literary representative of the Estate of John Masefield.

Page 14: William Jay Smith, *The Toaster*
From *Laughing Time: Nonsense Poems* by William Jay Smith, published by Delacorte Press, 1980
© 1955, 1957, 1980 William Jay Smith
Reproduced by permission of William Jay Smith.

Page 21: Rachmaninoff, Piano Concerto No. 2 (3rd mvt)
© Copyright 1901 Hawkes & Son (London) Ltd
Reproduced by permission of Boosey & Hawkes Music Publishers Ltd.

Page 22: Elgar, *The Dream of Gerontius*
Reproduced for sale in France, Belgium, Spain & Italy by permission of Novello & Co. Ltd.